# JOHN & 1 JOHN

## A Unique Parallel Study

*Chip Ricks*

Tyndale House
Publishers, Inc.
Wheaton, Illinois

All Scripture quotes are from the *New International Version* unless otherwise specified.

Second printing, December 1983
Library of Congress Catalog Card Number 82-60015
ISBN 0-8423-1890-9, paper

Printed in the United States of America

# CONTENTS

# Instructions for the Leader

The Bible is a powerful book. Because it is God's word to us, its truths can never be exhausted. This is why we can approach it in many ways and gain deeper understanding and new insights each time. Like a beautiful diamond, as you examine it from different perspectives, the Bible shines with new beauty in each angle of light.

Even though few critics would disagree that the Bible is the greatest literature ever written, many of us ignore the sensitive study of characters, the carefully chosen dialogue, and the deeply embedded theme of the authors, and go right to the interpretation.

This study will try to encourage you to look more carefully—not only to see the obvious, the literal, but to search beneath the surface to examine with a critical eye the truths John teaches through symbols and themes.

The study is inductive. Given the proper tools, we all learn in greater depth those things which we dig out for ourselves. The discussion leader is a guide—not a lecturer. The Discussion Leader's Guide in the back of this book will provide you with objectives, background information, and visual aid suggestions for each of the lessons. The Weekly Bible Study Guide is for the student's use as well as your reference. As members of the group discover for themselves the facts and truths in each lesson, these aids will help you to focus the discussion on the major theme expressed in the title. John uses these themes to accomplish his clearly stated purposes in John 20:31 and 1 John 5:13.

Your authority is God's Word. And your favorite questions may soon become, "In what verse did you see that?" or "Can you show me in the lesson exactly what gave you that idea?"

By using this literary-inductive approach you may well find that many in your group will develop fresh interests in an old, old story.

## How to Prepare to Lead a Group Study

1. Pray earnestly that the Holy Spirit will guide you as you study and as you lead the discussion.
2. Read through each lesson in both sections to give you an overview.
3. Study the lesson material in the Weekly Bible Study Guide just as those in your group will be doing. Write all the answers to the questions in a notebook. As you study the lesson, look up words you do not understand in a good dictionary.
4. Study the objectives and background information given for each lesson in the Discussion Leader's Guide. Focus on the title (which reflects the theme) and the objectives and get a good grasp of their relationship to the content. Remember: This material is to be used to answer questions, to clarify issues, to stimulate discussions. It should never be *read* to the group. Just share what you have learned from your study.
5. Look back over the questions for the lesson given in the Bible Study Guide and be sure you are prepared to guide the members of your group in finding the answers.

## How to Lead a Group Study

1. *Serve as a resource person to supply background material if needed.* This does not mean that you must be an authority on the Bible. You are not expected to have all the answers. Background material provided for each lesson, in the Discussion Leader's Guide, along with your careful preparation, should be sufficient.

2. *Raise questions for discussion.* You are not to lecture or teach. You are to ask questions. Members of the group will learn much more if they discover for themselves what the Bible says. Questions in the *Bible Study Guide* are focused on the theme, but you will want to spend more time on those which members of the group were unable to answer clearly in their individual study.

3. *Guide the discussion.* Answers to questions should be given by members of the group from the facts they observe in the assigned reading in John and 1 John and from their ideas about its meaning and application. Learning will take place through active participation of the members. To be sure this is happening, guide the discussion by asking questions. These suggestions may help:

a. If someone gives an unclear answer:
Leader: "What verses in your reading led you to that conclusion?"

b. If the question has been only partially answered:
Leader: "What else do you see in the reading?" "What else?" "Is there something more we've missed?"

c. If the response of a member is clearly inaccurate:
Leader: "That's an interesting observation, but does anyone else have a different idea?"

d. If someone dominates the discussion:
Leader: "On this next question, let's hear from someone who hasn't yet had a chance to contribute to the discussion."

e. If someone leads the discussion into an area unrelated to the question:
Leader: "I wish we had time to discuss that, because it's interesting, but we must get back to the question."

f. If a question arises which evokes the interest of the group but no one can answer:
Leader: "None of us seems to have the answer to that. Would someone like to do some research and give us a short report next time we meet?" Or say, "I'll see what I can find out about that and report back next time we meet." (Be sure to follow through.)

g. If someone brings up a personal problem which cannot be solved quickly:

Leader: "Could you and I get together later? I may be able to help you or suggest someone who can." (Be sure to follow through.)

h. Encourage discussion by acknowledging responses. A nod of your head expresses agreement. Or say, "That's a good thought," or, "Thank you. I hadn't thought of that," or, "Isn't that interesting?"

4. *Summarize the discussion at the end of the session.* You may do this yourself by listing four or five conclusions the group has reached about the lesson topic. Hopefully these will center around the objectives for the lesson. Or you may ask the group to summarize the discussion. Suggest that each member state one thing learned from the lesson.

**Suggestions for the First Group Meeting**

1. Spend time in prayer before your group arrives.

2. Greet your guests at the door. Be informal. Try to make them feel comfortable and relaxed.

3. Have name tags ready.

4. Begin the meeting on time. Explain that you will also close the meeting on time. This will allow members to plan their time and know that they can depend on you to keep your commitment.

5. Continue to create a relaxed atmosphere as you proceed. To help members of the group become more open with each other, suggest that they each answer the following questions:

a. What is your name and something unique about yourself? (Example: "I was the oldest of fifteen children." "I was born in Alaska." "I've never had a traffic ticket.")

b. What do you hope to get out of this study?

c. What is your very first memory of God?

As leader, begin with yourself. This will give others an example of the kind of answers you want and will make them more willing to share with the group. Answer the first question, and then let each member of the group answer before you continue with the next question. Be brief. Listen carefully as answers are given. Your goal is to get to know each member personally.

6. Hand out the books. Have members turn to the Introduc-

tion. Talk about John's purpose in writing the Gospel and letter, and ask someone to read John 30:31 and 1 John 5:13. A brief discussion may follow. You might ask such questions as these: What kinds of doubts have you had at some time in your life about Jesus Christ? What kinds of doubts have you had about eternal life? Summarize the discussion by stating that John recognized that doubting God's Word is a very human weakness. But he also understood that God does not want us to be unsure of who he is or of eternal life. John wrote his books that we might *believe* that Jesus is the Son of God and that we might *know* we have eternal life.

7. Continue by explaining the plan chosen for use of the *Bible Study Guide.* Talk about "Preparations for Individual Study," found in the Introduction, and then have members turn to Lesson 1. Explain what you will study at your next meeting.

8. Discuss briefly the section of the Introduction, "About the Man John." Have the group locate all of John's works in their Bibles.

9. Close the meeting with prayer.

10. You may wish to serve a light dessert and give the members of the group time to get better acquainted.

## Suggested Format for Group Meetings, Lessons 1-11, Plan 1, John and 1 John

1. Greet members of the group at the door. Create a warm, friendly atmosphere.
2. Have name tags by the door.
3. Follow a time plan.

*First hour:* If the group has as many as twelve people, break into two groups for discussion of study questions on John. For each six people, create another group with a discussion leader. Leaders should open with prayer, asking that God will bless the time of study.

*Ten-minute break.*

*Second hour:* Bring everyone together for the study of 1 John. Ask someone to read the lesson from 1 John. Give background information from the *Discussion Leader's Guide* if you feel it would be helpful at this time. Work through the study questions together, making use of any visual aids suggested—or any that you plan yourself. Close with prayer, thanking God for the learning and fellowship that has occurred.

### Suggestions for Single Book Study

If you are studying only John or 1 John, you may not need a two-hour time plan. Select any ideas that are helpful to you from the suggestions made for both hours and adapt them to the needs of your group.

### Suggested Format for the Last Meeting: Our Fellowship, in Jesus

This should be a time to enjoy the fellowship which will surely have grown as you study the books of John. A shared luncheon or dinner is a good way to close the study. After eating, plan group singing and a time for each member to share some of the things learned from the study. Spend a few minutes summarizing what it means to *believe* that Jesus is the Son of God, and what it means to *know* that you have eternal life. Before you separate as a group, have a time of prayer to thank God for all that he has taught you.

# Introduction

**Purpose**

The books of John and 1 John complement each other and can profitably be studied together. Note John's purpose in writing them:

*These are recorded so* that you will believe *that he is the Messiah, the Son of God, and that believing in him you will have life.* John 20:31 (TLB)

*I have written this to you who believe in the Son of God so* that you may know *you have eternal life.* 1 John 5:13 (TLB)

THAT YOU WILL *BELIEVE.*

THAT YOU MAY *KNOW.*

The word *believe* appears ninety-eight times in the book of John. The word *know* appears thirty times in the short letter, 1 John.

To accomplish his purposes in both works, John presents Jesus as the Word of life, the Light in a world of darkness. He is God, who came to draw us to himself through love. As his children we are commanded to love each other. We are warned against false teaching and pointed toward Jesus, the Spirit of Truth, who through perfect love for us, has given us eternal life.

In studying the two books together, we find that one book reinforces the other. For those just beginning to seek the truth about Jesus Christ, the study offers an opportunity to find answers. For those Christians who have doubts, or who need encouragement, the study offers an opportunity to firm up beliefs and make stronger commitments to Jesus Christ. To all who dare to give the time, John and 1 John offer a challenge to *believe* and to *know*.

## Plans for Use of the Study Guide

Ideally, this study requires a commitment of thirty minutes, four days a week for individual study, and a two-hour commitment one day a week for group study, for a total of eleven weeks. However, these lessons can be used in a number of alternate ways.

*Plan 1. Individual and Group Study of John and 1 John Together:* Each of eleven lessons consists of four thirty-minute studies in John and one study in 1 John. A group may elect to meet weekly for two hours. The first hour can be used for the John studies, completed individually prior to the group meeting. Answers to the questions can be shared and help given with any problems encountered. The second hour can be used for study of 1 John together. This group meeting can be scheduled anytime: on Sunday morning as a Sunday school class, or during the week—day or evening. A group session during the twelfth week for review and fellowship completes the study. Suggestions and helps for discussion leaders are given in Instructions for the Leader.

*Plan 2. Individual Study in John:* Four individual studies are planned for each of eleven lessons to take you through John. These can be self-paced but will be more helpful if at least one lesson is completed weekly.

*Plan 3. Individual Study in 1 John:* Eleven lessons are planned on 1 John and are found in Study 5. These are complete in themselves and follow the theme in the title of each lesson.

*Plan 4. Group Study in John:* A group may elect to study only John, coming together weekly to discuss the questions provided in the eleven lessons. If the members of the group prepare the studies at home, the group discussions will be more effective. Help in leading group discussions is found in Instructions for the Leader.

*Plan 5. Group Study in 1 John:* A group may elect to study only 1 John, meeting weekly for teaching and discussion. Members of the group may do as little or as much preparation for the study as they have time. Suggestions for discussion leaders are also provided.

### Preparations for Individual Study

1. Try to set aside the same time each day for prayer and study. It is your "quiet time," a time to open your heart to the Lord and allow him to speak to you through his Word. An early morning time is best for many people and sets a pattern of quiet resolve for the day. A time at the end of a busy day is best for others—a time to relax, to enjoy learning, to evaluate past events. Whatever your choice of time, give it top priority.
2. Find a quiet place. This may be a favorite chair in the corner of your bedroom, a pillow tossed on the floor in the living room, a chair at the dining room table. While we know God is everywhere, having a place set aside especially for reserved time with him is helpful.
3. Pray for the guidance of the Holy Spirit before you begin.
4. Read through the Scripture portion.
5. Read through the questions.
6. Reread the Scripture with the questions in mind.
7. Keep a notebook and write down in it the answers to the questions. Use a dictionary to look up any words which need further clarification. Circle those questions which you cannot clearly answer. Watch for answers in future studies. If you are in a study group, discussion with others will help.
8. As you complete each study, place a check in the square provided: □ Study 1.
9. Thank the Lord for what you have learned from the study, and ask him to help you apply what he has taught you.

### About the Man John

John, the beloved disciple of our Lord, is the author of a biography of Jesus titled the Gospel according to John, as well as three letters—1, 2, and 3 John, and the book of Revelation. John wrote his Gospel and letters around A.D. 85-90, approximately twenty years after the Apostle Paul died. Later, around A.D. 90-95, Revelation was written. Authorities agree that John's works were the last of our Bible to be completed, and most authorities believe John's books are the only ones written after the fall of Jerusalem in A.D. 70.

Just what do we know about the man John, who in his mature years wrote down the last words of Jesus to be recorded in our Bible?

John was one of the first disciples to be called by Jesus (Mark 1:19, 20), and he remained with him throughout his ministry. In studying John's Gospel, we learn that John was an ambitious, intolerant, boisterous man when he first met Jesus. But walking close to the Lord, being taught by him, John grew. His attitudes, values, direction in life all changed. John became the "dearly beloved disciple"; his life became the very embodiment of love. In his Gospel he clearly attributed these changes to his Lord Jesus Christ. And of all Jesus' disciples, John was the one chosen by the Lord to care for his mother after his death on the cross (John 19:26, 27).

Once Jesus ascended to heaven, John's motivation for living was to share all he had learned about the Lord. His name, with Peter's, headed the list of apostles (Acts 1:13). Again with Peter, he healed the lame man at the gate (Acts 3), following what he had been taught by Jesus. Later John appeared before the Sanhedrin with Peter (Acts 4:1-13) and then accompanied him to Samaria (Acts 8:14). While Peter went on to establish churches, John's work was apparently of a more comtemplative nature.

We don't know when or how John left Jerusalem, but possibly he wrote the Gospel of John and 1, 2, and 3 John at Ephesus where he pastored the Christian church. From there John was taken and imprisoned on an island called Patmos in the Aegean Sea during persecution of Christians by the Roman Emperor, Domitian. There he wrote the book of Revelation.

John's writings seem to reveal his deep perception of the innermost thoughts and emotions of the Lord. And, after years of living the Christian life, perhaps he understood more than any other writer the teachings of Jesus concerning sin and forgiveness, the help of the indwelling Holy Spirit, and the tender love of the Lord who calls us to full commitment.

*Weekly Bible Study Guide*

# ONE

# Jesus: The Word of Life

*John 1—3; 1 John 1:1-4*

*O Word of God Incarnate*
*O Wisdom from on high,*
*O Truth unchanged, unchanging,*
*O Light of our dark sky:*
*We praise Thee for the radiance*
*That from the hallowed page,*
*A lantern to our footsteps,*
*Shines on from age to age.*

William How

☐ **Study 1**

*Reading: John 1:1-34*

1. Make a list of the facts given about the Word in verses 1-4.
2. What kind of connection is made in verses 1-4 between the Word and men?
3. Who is John and how is his relationship to the light explained in verses 6 and 7? (Note: This John, who came to be known as John the Baptist, is not the man who wrote this book.) What relationship do you see between the Word in verse 1 and the light in verses 7 and 8?

4. Verse 14 adds another dimension to the Word. As you understand this, what was the purpose of the Word becoming flesh, explained more fully in verses 9-18?
5. Compare verses 7, 23, and 31. What additional information is given about the mission of John the Baptist in relation to the Word?
6. Trace the name changes of the Word starting with verse 1. Make a list. What evidence do you see that this Jesus in verses 29-34 is the Word of verse 1?

☐ **Study 2**

*Reading: John 1:35-51*

1. Note the response of each of the four disciples in verses 35-50 to Jesus. What caused each of them to follow Jesus?
2. Go through verses 35-51 in chapter 1 and add to your list of all the names now given to the Word. Why do you think the author uses so many different titles?
3. Beside each name on your list, write down what the name means to you personally.
4. Why do you think Jesus changed Simon's name? (See verse 42.)
5. From your observation of Jesus in verses 35-51, what three words would you use to describe the ways in which he relates to people?

☐ **Study 3**

*Reading: John 2*

1. Verses 1-11 record the first of the "miraculous signs" in John's Gospel. What relationship do you see between this "sign" and John's writing objective stated in John 20:31?
2. What does Jesus do to perform this miraculous sign?
3. List the verbs in verses 7-10 which reveal what Jesus tells the servants to do. Now list the verbs which show the response of the servants to Jesus' words. What can you learn from this?
4. From a study of the story in verses 12-25, what do you learn about the authority of Jesus?
5. The words of Jesus in verses 19-22 are strange. Why do you think he refers to his body as a "temple"? Is there any evidence

that the disciples have any better understanding of Jesus' words than the Jews do?

6. Compare the responses of the people in verses 12-25 with the response of the servants in verses 1-11. With whom do you identify?

☐ **Study 4**

*Reading: John 3*

1. Why do you think Nicodemus, a learned man, has difficulty understanding the words of Jesus?
2. Twice Jesus says, "I tell you the truth . . ." (verses 3 and 5). Why does he repeat this phrase? Immediately after, Jesus talks about being "born of the Spirit." What is your understanding of that phrase? What choice does Jesus lay before Nicodemus?
3. Many incidents in the Bible are a foreshadowing of things to come and often have deeper meaning than the incident itself. In verses 14 and 15 Jesus recalls such an incident recorded in Numbers 21:4-9. Compare the two Scripture passages. What is Jesus revealing about himself?
4. Read verse 16 as a personal message: "For God so loved *me* that he gave his only Son that I, who believe in him, shall not perish but have eternal life." Apply verses 17 and 18 to yourself as well. How does this make you feel? Do you believe Jesus' words?
5. In verses 19-21 darkness and light are contrasted. What moves a person from darkness to light?
6. In what ways do the words of John the Baptist (verses 27-36) and the words of Jesus (verses 10-21) agree in this chapter?

☐ **Study 5**

*Reading: 1 John 1:1-4*

1. How has John come to know Jesus, the Word of life?
2. Note that John uses both the word "seen" and the word "looked" in verse 1. The Greek word for "see" means "a steadfast or searching look." Specifically, what do you think John means by "a steadfast or searching look" at Jesus? In what ways can this be applied to our getting to know Jesus today?
3. The word "fellowship" comes from the Greek word *koinonia,*

meaning to share something in common. What more can you learn about fellowship from verses 1-4?

4. Is there anyone in your life with whom you have this kind of fellowship?
5. With whom did John say he has fellowship? What is his desire for you? How would you describe the quality of your fellowship?

### Lesson 1 Overview

1. Look back over the studies in Lesson 1. In what ways does the reading in 1 John reinforce what you learned about Jesus in John 1-3?

2. As you have studied Lesson 1, some questions may have come to your mind which still have not been answered. Write these down. As you continue your study in John and 1 John, watch for answers.

# TWO

# Jesus: The Light in Fellowship

*John 4—5; 1 John 1:5-10*

*The Lord is my light and my salvation; whom shall I fear?*

Psalm 27:1 (TLB)

☐ **Study 1**

*Reading: John 4:1-42*

1. The Samaritan woman is surprised that Jesus, a Jew, speaks to her. But what evidence do you have that Jesus is unconcerned about the traditional prejudice? What *does* concern Jesus? (See verses 8-10.)
2. What are the requirements for entering into fellowship with Jesus as you understand them from verse 10?
3. In verse 14, what are the promises of Jesus? What do you think he means?
4. What hinders the Samaritan woman as she tries to understand the words of Jesus? Note the dialogue in verses 10-15.
5. As the story progresses, what changes do you begin to see in the Samaritan woman? What evidence is there that the light is penetrating her darkness? (See verses 16-30.)
6. What is the difference between the fellowship the disciples are

talking about and the fellowship Jesus is talking about in verses 31-38?

7. Note carefully the reaction of the Samaritan woman now that she has experienced fellowship with Jesus. Describe her response. In what ways is the light shining in darkness? (See verses 39-42.)
8. Think back to the time you first began to realize who Jesus was. Write down what you remember about your questions and realizations. Do you think you felt anything like the Samaritan woman?

### □ Study 2

*Reading: John 4:43-54*

1. Not everyone wants to have fellowship with Jesus. Note the response of the two groups of people in verses 44 and 45. What kinds of responses do you see to Jesus today?
2. What are the verbs in verse 47 which tell the response of the nobleman to Jesus?
3. The nobleman is concerned that his son may die, and he pleads with Jesus to save his life. Jesus does more than give the son life. In what way does he also give the father life? What responses enable this man to receive new life? (See verses 50-53.)
4. Verse 54 states that this is the second miraculous sign Jesus performed—both in Cana in Galilee. Compare the response of the servants to Jesus' words in John 2:8 with the response of the nobleman in this story. How should you respond to Jesus' words?
5. From your study of verses 43-54, what conclusions can you draw about the relationship of response to Jesus and fellowship with him?
6. What three words best describe your fellowship with Jesus? Are you satisfied with your part in maintaining this fellowship?

### □ Study 3

*Reading: John 5:1-18*

1. Study the question Jesus asks in verse 6 and the answer the invalid gives in verse 7. What do you learn about the invalid from his response to Jesus' question?

2. What do you learn about Jesus' words and the man's response to those words in verses 8 and 9? How does this lesson apply to you?
3. Look closely at verses 10-15. Do you think it was a coincidence that Jesus found the man in the Temple? Support your answer.
4. In verses 16-18 two controversial issues arise. The first concerns the keeping of the Sabbath. Look up Exodus 20:8. How do you feel about Jesus' resolution of this issue? What kinds of things do you feel comfortable doing on the Lord's Day? What kinds of things would you not feel comfortable doing?
5. The second issue which arises in verses 16-18 concerns Jesus' relationship to God. Jesus calls him "Father." What did this mean to the Jews? What does it mean to you?

☐ **Study 4**

*Reading: John 5:19-47*

1. Jesus describes his relationship to the Father in verses 19-30. Study this relationship by listing in two columns (one headed "Jesus," the other "Father") the facts you learn about each from Jesus' words.
2. What do you see as the ingredients of the fellowship Jesus enjoyed with his Father? What do you learn from this?
3. Carefully read verse 24 printed below in grammatical structure from the *New International Version.*

| *Subject* | *Verb* | *Objects* |
|---|---|---|
| I | tell | you the truth: |
| whoever | hears | my word and |
| | believes | him who sent me |
| | has | eternal life and |
| | will not be condemned; | |
| he | has crossed over | from death to life. |

Now look at the subject "whoever." Does this include you? Note the pronoun "he" which substitutes for "whoever" in the latter part of the sentence. Next look at the tense of all verbs. Past, present, and future tenses are all used in this sentence. Do a close study of the objects of these verbs in relation to the verb tenses. Write down the things you learn.

4. What relationship does "darkness to light" have to the phrase "death to life" found in verse 24?
5. While Jewish law only required two testimonies in a court of law, Jesus discusses five testimonies to his truth in verses 31-46. Why was each one of these a valid witness to the Jews? Do you feel that these witnesses to the identity of Jesus are valid for you today?
6. Those people Jesus addresses in verses 37b-47 are not in his fellowship. List the reasons Jesus gives why this is so. In what ways are these same reasons keeping people from Jesus today?

☐ **Study 5**

*Reading: 1 John 1:5-10*

1. In Scripture "light" and "life" belong to Jesus and his kingdom. "Darkness" and "death" belong to Satan and his kingdom. Study verses 5-7. Is there any evidence in these verses that there is a gray area, or are all people who are not in the light of Jesus' fellowship residing in the darkness of Satan's kingdom?
2. If "God is Light" (verse 5), is he not also "truth"? Then, if we do not believe Jesus' words, can we have fellowship with him? Do you think a person who is not a believer can have fellowship with a person who is? Think about your own life. Can your answers to these questions be verified from your experiences?
3. See what you can learn from studying verses 6-10 set in parallel structure below (from the NIV) and listed under "Darkness" or "Light."

*Darkness*

If we claim to have fellowship with him yet walk in the darkness,<br>
  we lie and<br>
  do not live by the truth.<br>
If we claim to be without sin,<br>
  we deceive ourselves and<br>
  the truth is not in us.

If we claim we have not sinned,
we make him out to be a liar and
his word has no place in our lives.

*Light*
If we walk in the light as he is in the light,
we have fellowship with one another, and
the blood of Jesus, his Son, purifies us from every sin.
If we confess our sins,
he is faithful and just and will forgive us our sins and
purify us from all unrighteousness.

Do you see all the progressions which our actions cause? For example, note the progression deeper and deeper into darkness when we make false claims:

First: we claim to have fellowship with him
Next: we claim to be without sin
Then: we claim we have not sinned

The results of these false claims also follow a progression:

First: we lie
Next: we deceive ourselves
Then: we make him out to be a liar

What is the progression concerning truth? Follow through on the progressions under "Light."

4. Look back at question 1. Do you think that we can add "truth" to the kingdom of Jesus and "lies" to the kingdom of Satan?
5. Now that you have studied these verses carefully, try to sense the importance of John's message which he says he heard from Jesus: "God is light; in him there is no darkness at all." Write down any thoughts that occur to you.

## Lesson 2 Overview

1. Glance back through these five studies of Lesson 2 and make three lists: (a) the things you learned about Jesus, (b) the things you learned about light, and (c) the things you learned about fellowship.

2. Did you find answers to questions remaining from your overview of Lesson 1?

3. Write down any questions that have occurred to you and have not been answered during your study of Lesson 2. As you continue your study of John and 1 John, watch for answers.

# THREE
# Jesus: Our Advocate

*John 6—7:24; 1 John 2:1-6*

*. . . There is someone to plead for you before the Father. His name is Jesus Christ, the one who is all that is good and who pleases God completely.*

1 John 2:1b (TLB)

□ **Study 1**

*Reading: John 6:1-15*

1. Take a close look at the crowd of people in this story. How would you describe them?
2. Why do you think the Jewish Passover Feast is mentioned in verse 4? What connection does it have with the lesson Jesus is about to teach the disciples?
3. Someday Jesus will be the disciples' advocate before the Father. Now, like a lawyer, he is preparing them for that day. Study Jesus' question in verses 5 and 6 and the disciples' answers in verses 7-9. What problems do you see?
4. Look beneath the "miraculous sign" which Jesus did in feeding the 5,000. Remember, he is teaching the disciples. What do you think Jesus wanted them to learn?

5. In verse 15, Jesus, "knowing that they intended to come and make him king by force, withdrew again into the hills by himself." What are other possible reasons why he left both the disciples and the crowd at this time? (See verses 1-14.)

### ☐ Study 2

*Reading: John 6:16-47*

1. In literature, the sea is traditionally a testing place—a place of judgment. (Remember the experiences of the Israelites and Pharaoh's army in crossing the Red Sea? The experience of Jonah in the sea?) What evidence can you see in verses 16-21 that the Sea of Galilee is serving this purpose?
2. Do you think fear is an appropriate response to Jesus? How is fear the opposite of faith?
3. A day has gone by, but we can sense that Jesus is still deeply concerned that no one understood the object lesson he taught when he fed the 5,000. Study the conversation—questions and answers—in verses 25-35. Jesus is presenting a strong argument for truth. Assume you are one of the Jews in the crowd. What are some of the questions you would ask at this point?
4. Compare God's gift of bread in the desert referred to in John 6:31 and explained more fully in Exodus 16:1-8, with Jesus' gift of bread referred to in John 6:35-43. Look at the responses of the forefathers and their descendants to these two gifts. In what ways are their responses similar?
5. What evidence do you see in verses 35-47 that Jesus is God, the Father's provision for the life of man? Why do you think the evidence as Jesus presents it does not satisfy the Jews?
6. On a scale of 1-10, from bread in the desert to the Bread of Life, how would you rate your response to Jesus' plea not to be concerned about perishable bread but rather to seek that which is eternal?

### ☐ Study 3

*Reading: John 6:48-71*

1. Jesus continues to use the symbol of bread to teach in verses 48-51. This symbol is well known to those Jews familiar with the

Scriptures. Read Deuteronomy 8:3 and Isaiah 55:2. How do these help your understanding of John 6:48-51?

2. Jesus goes farther with the bread symbol. In verse 51, Jesus says, "This Bread is my flesh." Follow through to verse 63. Here the symbol takes on additional meaning. What do you think Jesus is teaching?
3. Jesus is an advocate for men under sentence of death. He has driven his point home, and he offers life. But "this is a hard teaching. Who can accept it?" List the various responses of those who heard Jesus (verses 60-71).
4. Describe how you are responding to Jesus' words.

☐ **Study 4**

*Reading: John 7:1-24*

1. Picture this reading as a drama. Draw evidence from verses 1-24 to describe the brothers, the Jews, the crowd, and Jesus himself.
2. No one seems to believe Jesus—not even his own brothers (verse 5); the world hates him (verse 7); he is being falsely judged (verse 24). Yet what do you see in Jesus' character, as you examine verses 1-24, that keeps him moving toward his goal of changing man's sentence of death to a gift of eternal life?
3. What do you think "healing the whole man" means in verse 23? What implication does this have for you personally?

☐ **Study 5**

*Reading: 1 John 2:1-6*

1. In verses 1 and 2 John establishes a courtroom scene. Who is the judge? the advocate? the defendant? What is the charge? Picture the scene.
2. Remember this letter was written to believers. What do you see in verses 1 and 2 which indicates John's attitude toward believers who sin? What evidence do you see here that Jesus shares John's attitude?
3. In your own words, define sin. What things in your life do you believe to be sinful? Why do you think it is necessary that you have an advocate before the Father to take care of these sins?
4. John's teaching is clear: It is God's desire that Christians do not

sin. And John suggests that if we continually sin we may not be Christians. Study verses 3-6. List the characteristics of a Christian as John records them.

5. In what ways has God been speaking to you through his Word? Are you listening? Are you obeying his voice?

**Lesson 3 Overview**

1. Look back over the studies in Lesson 3. Clearly Jesus' mission to the world was to become our advocate before the Father. How do you feel about God's plan to accept only one advocate in his court? See: Romans 3:21-24 and Acts 4:12. In what ways is this a "hard teaching" for man?

2. Did you find answers to your questions remaining from Lesson 2? Write down any unanswered questions you have about Lesson 3. As you continue your study of John and 1 John, watch for answers.

# FOUR

# Love: The New Commandment

*John 7:25—8:59; 1 John 2:7-17*

*"And so I am giving a new commandment to you now—love each other just as much as I love you. Your strong love for each other will prove to the world that you are my disciples."*

John 13:34, 35 (TLB)

□ **Study 1**

*Reading: John 7:25-52*

1. What evidence of Jesus' love for mankind can you find in his actions recorded in verses 25-52? What do you believe to be his deep concerns?
2. Study Jesus' teaching in verses 28, 29, 33, 34, 37, and 38. What can you learn about the character of Jesus from his words?
3. List the various reactions of the people who heard Jesus teach in the Temple court (verses 25-52). What do you see as some of the reasons why many refused to believe that Jesus was indeed the Christ? How do you hear these reasons being expressed today?
4. In verses 38 and 39 Jesus offers the wonderful promise of the Holy Spirit to all who believe in him. Just what do Jesus' words mean to you when he describes the Holy Spirit as "streams of living water" that will "flow from within"?

5. Think of the love of Jesus—a love that would send his Holy Spirit to live in man. Yet his words of promise divided the people (verses 40-44). What evidence do you see today that Jesus' words divide people?
6. What evidence do you see in verses 45-52 that the Pharisees, spiritual leaders of their day, did not know how to love either God or man?

☐ **Study 2**

*Reading: John 8:1-11*

1. How do you see Jesus' love demonstrated in this story?
2. What words would you use to describe the actions and attitudes of the teachers of the law and the Pharisees?
3. What kind of response do you think Jesus' love evoked in the woman?
4. What kind of thoughts do you think Jesus' love evoked in the accusers?
5. Recall a time when you did something wrong and someone responded to you with loving forgiveness. In what ways did the person's response affect you?

☐ **Study 3**

*Reading: John 8:12-30*

1. Jesus was still teaching in the Temple court. During this time, the Feast of Tabernacles, the Temple was brilliantly lighted to commemorate God's guidance of the Israelites through the wilderness by a cloud which looked like fire at night. Read Numbers 9:15-17. What new insights do these verses give to help you better understand Jesus' claim and promise in John 8:12?
2. What testimony do you see in verses 13-18 that Jesus is indeed the Son of God?
3. Make a list of all the things that Jesus says about the Pharisees in verses 14-21. What conclusions can you draw from your list?
4. Note the chasm that separates Jesus and the Jews in verses 21-24. What significance do these verses have for us today?

5. What does Jesus mean in verse 28 when he says, "When you have lifted up the Son of Man, then you will know who I am"?

☐ **Study 4**

*Reading: John 8:31-59*

1. What do you think Jesus meant when he acknowledged to the Jews that they were Abraham's "descendants" but denied that they were Abraham's "children"? (See verses 31-41.)
2. Again Jesus' words divide the Jews as he talks about two families: the family of God and the family of the devil. What distinguishing factors do you find in verses 31-47?
3. What evidence can you find in verses 31-47 that God loves us and wants us in his family?
4. Do a close study of the verb "hear" as it is used in verses 38-40, 43, and 47. What truths can you learn from this?
5. What is the relationship between the "word" and the "life"? (See verses 48-59.) Why is it important that we understand this relationship?

☐ **Study 5**

*Reading: 1 John 2:7-17*

1. Read John 13:34-35 again. In what ways do these verses help you to understand 1 John 2:7-11?
2. What do you see as the differences between those who walk in darkness and those who walk in light? Do you think those who walk in darkness can obey Jesus' commandment to love others as he loves us?
3. Verses 12-14 are specifically directed to those in God's family. What are some of the things you learn about yourself from these verses?
4. What does the command in verse 15 mean to you personally? Does your understanding of this verse pose any problem with your understanding of John 3:16?
5. In verses 15-17 John touches on the three areas of temptation common to man: cravings of sinful man (body), lust of the eyes (soul, emotions), and boasting of what he has and does (spirit). In what ways has God's love affected your attitude toward these desires?

## Lesson 4 Overview

1. Until men saw love incarnate in Jesus Christ, they did not really know what love could be. Look back over the readings in Lesson 4. In what ways do you see the love of God expressed?

2. We have been commanded to love others just as much as Jesus loves us. As you think about the actions and words of Jesus in this lesson, try to translate the commandment into your life. Why do you think Jesus would give us a commandment that is so difficult for us to obey?

3. Check the unanswered questions you had following Lesson 3. Did you find answers? Write down any questions you still have about Lesson 4. Watch for answers as you continue your study.

# FIVE

# God's Children: Their Choices and Dangers

*John 9—11:46; 1 John 2:18-29*

*"I have set before you life or death, blessing or curse. Oh, that you would choose life; that you and your children might live! Choose to love the Lord your God and to obey him and to cling to him, for he is your life and the length of your days."*

Deuteronomy 30:19, 20 (TLB)

☐ **Study 1**

*Reading: John 9*

1. Compare the question of sin treated in verses 1-3 with Jesus' admonition of the man he healed at the pool of Bethsaida found in John 5:14. What conclusions can you draw from these verses about sin and physical affliction?
2. Examine verses 4 and 5 carefully. What connection is Jesus making between light-darkness and day-night? What choice and what danger does Jesus lay before the disciples? How do you think this choice and this danger apply to you?
3. Study the verbs in verse 7 which indicate Jesus' commands and the blind man's responses. What can be learned from this?
4. While the physical healing of the blind man is recorded in verse 7, the spiritual healing is not complete until verse 38. Look closely

at all intervening verses. List the choices and dangers that this man faced before he could say "Lord, I believe" and John could write that "he worshiped him."

5. While the parents of the blind man faced essentially the same choices as their son, they responded differently. How do you feel about the parents and their responses? (See verses 18-23.) What application does this have to our lives today?
6. In verse 39, Jesus explains the judgment men face because his light shines in the world: those who acknowledge their blindness will see; those who assert that they are not blind, will indeed remain blind. Trace the actions and words of the Pharisees from verse 13 to verse 41 where Jesus says to them, "Now that you claim you can see, your guilt remains." What can you discover as the primary reason they could not be healed of their blindness? What does this have to do with the "guilt" Jesus refers to in verse 41?

☐ **Study 2**

*Reading: John 10:1-21*

1. Jesus is using figurative language (verse 6) to teach an important truth. Identify the good shepherd, the thief and robber, and the sheep.
2. Make a list of the verbs in verses 1-6 which tell us the actions of the good shepherd, the thief, and the sheep. Notice that the sheep respond in three ways to the shepherd and in three ways to the thief. What are some of the things you learned from a study of these verbs?
3. In verses 7-10 Jesus uses another metaphor to describe his purpose. What additional understanding of Jesus is given when he says, "I am the gate"? What meaning is conveyed by the verbs in verse 9 which describe the actions of those who enter through the "gate"?
4. Study the purpose and actions of the thief in verses 10-13 by listing the action verbs relating to him. Contrast this thief with the good shepherd described in verses 14-18.
5. Why do you think the "Jews were again divided" (verses 19-21)? What choice did they face? What danger?

☐ **Study 3**

*Reading: John 10:22-42*

1. Examine the words and actions of the Jews in verses 22-33. What evidence do you see that they have chosen to go the way of the thief and robber rather than follow the good shepherd?
2. Study the statements Jesus makes in verses 27-30. What does each one mean to you personally?
3. Read Psalm 82 in which the judges of Israel, God's representatives, are called "gods" and "sons of the Most High." Compare this Scripture reference to the words of Jesus in John 10:34-38. What evidence is presented to prove that God's Son is far greater than the judges who were called "gods"?
4. Why do you think the people across the Jordan chose to believe Jesus when the Jews in Jerusalem did not? (See verses 40-42.)

☐ **Study 4**

*Reading: John 11:1-46*

1. In John 9, Jesus healed a blind man. In John 11, Jesus raised Lazarus from the dead. Compare the purposes of these two works expressed in John 9:3 and 11:4. What evidence can you give that God can be glorified through our physical disabilities and limitations even today?
2. Note that the theme of darkness and light is present in both stories. Compare John 9:4, 5 with 11:9-14 and then study 11:37. In what ways does the second story serve as a progressively stronger symbol of Jesus' work to bring the Jews from darkness to light?
3. Do you think the Jews' choice to remain in darkness rather than come to the light was also a choice of death rather than life?
4. What choices are made by Mary, Martha, and their friends? (Note particularly verses 25, 27, 32, 45, and 46). What evidence is there in your life and the lives of your friends that similar choices are still being made today?

☐ **Study 5**

*Reading: 1 John 2:18-29*

1. What interrelationships of ideas do you see between John's

words in verses 18 and 19 concerning the "last hour" and Jesus' statements in John 9:4, 5 and 11:9, 10 concerning "day and night"? In what ways do the truths in these verses affect your life today?

2. What does "anointing from the Holy One" mean to you (verse 20)? What additional information is provided in verse 27? Check the concordance of your Bible to see ways in which the word "anointing" has been used in other books of the Old and New Testaments.
3. How do you reconcile John's statement in verse 27 that "you do not need anyone to teach you" with Jesus' command in Matthew 28:19, 20?
4. Twice in verses 20 and 21 John asserts that the recipients of this letter "know the truth." Study verses 22-25. The majority of the Jews of Jesus' time acknowledged the God of Abraham, but denied his Son, Jesus. What do you see as the danger of such a choice? Do you think this danger is present today for those who believe in God but deny Jesus Christ?

**Lesson 5 Overview**

1. Reread the selection from Deuteronomy 30:19, 20 at the beginning of this lesson. What new insights have you gained from the study of Lesson 5 which help you better understand the choice between life or death set before the people by Moses in his speech? How does this choice affect you personally?

2. Think about the deep love of Jesus Christ manifested in his actions and words as you studied them in Lesson 4. What evidence can you give from Lesson 5 that the character of Jesus is consistent with the choices placed before man?

3. Do you have any unanswered questions remaining from previous lessons? Jot down any new questions resulting from the study of Lesson 5 and watch for answers as you continue in John and 1 John.

# SIX

# God's Children: Striving for Obedience

*John 11:47—13:32; 1 John 3:1-10*

*The road to faith passes through obedience to the call of Jesus.*

Dietrich Bonhoeffer
(*The Cost of Discipleship*, p. 68)

□ **Study 1**

*Reading: John 11:47—12:19*

1. Do a character study of the chief priests and Pharisees by studying their words and actions in 11:47-57. Is there any evidence in these verses that they knew Jesus was the expected Messiah but chose to oppose him?
2. What do you understand the prophecy of Caiaphas (verses 49-52) to mean?
3. The word "obey" comes from the Latin word *obedire*, meaning "to give ear," "to hear." It also translates into English as "to comply." Could not our obedience to Jesus, then, be tested by how well we "listen" to his words and "comply" with his teaching? Using this criteria as you study 12:1-11, test the obedience of the group gathered around Jesus: Lazarus, Martha, Mary, Judas Iscariot, the chief priests, and "many of the Jews."

Would you agree that hearing Jesus always brings some kind of response?

4. Underline the verb "heard" in verses 12 and 18. Now list the verbs in verses 12-19 which indicate what the crowd did when they heard that Jesus was coming and that he had raised Lazarus from the dead. Do you think their response to what they had heard was a response of obedience?

☐ **Study 2**

*Reading: John 12:20-50*

1. List the words in verses 23-36 which have to do with time. How do these words affect this reply which comes from Jesus as a response to the request of the Greeks to see him (verses 20-22). What do you think is the connection between the request and the response?
2. Examine verses 24-26 carefully. Specifically, what application do these words have to your life?
3. In verses 32-34, for the third time in John's Gospel, Jesus refers to his coming death on the cross. Write down the purpose of Jesus' obedience unto death expressed in all three references: John 3:14, 15; 8:28; 12:32-34. What relationship do you see between Jesus' death and our obedience to death called for in verses 24-26?
4. Note the theme of light and darkness which appears again in verses 35, 36, and 46. How do these relate to obedience? How do they relate to "the hour"?
5. Circle the word "believe" in verses 37-50. In what ways does Bonhoeffer's statement, "The road to faith passes through obedience to the call of Jesus," support Jesus' teaching about believing in him?
6. In verse 47 the verbs "hear" and "keep" could fulfill our definition of "obey." What evidence do you see in verses 47-50 that our response to Jesus' words is of vital importance?

☐ **Study 3**

*Reading: John 13:1-17*

1. What relationship, if any, do you see between the story recorded in 12:1-7 and Jesus' decision to wash the disciples' feet in 13:1-7?

2. Jesus had consistently manifested his love for the disciples, yet John says in verse 1 that, "He now showed them the *full extent* of his love." What things do you learn about our Lord's love from verses 2-12 which might help you to understand what John meant?
3. What lessons in obedience are taught in verses 13-17? List some specific ways in which you believe Jesus would have you carry out these lessons in obedience.

☐ **Study 4**

*Reading: John 13:18-32*

1. For a long time Judas had lived with Jesus and heard his teachings just as the other eleven disciples had. Yet his response was far different. Trace the work of Satan on his heart in John 6:70, 71, 12:4-6, and 13:18-30. What evidence do you find that a growing disobedience led eventually to his betrayal of Jesus?
2. Study verses 21-30. Note questions, answers, responses. What can you learn about the eleven disciples from this? What can you learn about Judas?
3. Study each word in verse 30. In what ways does John's choice of words deepen the impact of Judas' betrayal—the ultimate in disobedience to Jesus?
4. In what way can man choose this ultimate disobedience to Jesus today?
5. Study Jesus' use of the verb "glorify" in verses 31 and 32. What do you think the word means? Why do you think Jesus is emphasizing the word at this point in time?

☐ **Study 5**

*Reading: 1 John 3:1-10*

1. What characteristics of God are revealed in verses 1-3 which would make you want to love and obey him even if you knew nothing more about him?
2. Circle the word "sin" in verses 4-9. The Greek form of the verb used in these verses means "to practice sinning" or "to habitually sin." (Verse 6 clarifies the meaning of the verb "sin.") How do

you feel when you sin against the God you described in question 1? Do you think believers can habitually sin against God?

3. What evidence can you find in verses 7-10 that a division exists between those who obey God and those who do not?

### Lesson 6 Overview

1. As you look back over the lesson, what evidence do you see that there were many people who were searching for someone who could meet their needs—spiritual as well as physical? Why do you think so many of these were unwilling to obey the one who could fulfill their needs completely? What application of your findings can be made to people today?

2. In what specific areas of your life do you find obedience to Jesus most difficult? Why do you think you find it hard to obey at all times?

3. Do you have any questions remaining from previous lessons which are still unanswered? What new questions do you have from Lesson 6? Write these down and watch for answers as you continue your study.

# SEVEN

# God's Children: Learning to Love

*John 13:33—15:17; 1 John 3:11-24*

*You will find, my child, that love rarely ever reaches out to save except it does it with a broken hand.*

Calvin Miller
(*The Singer*, pp. 142, 143)

☐ **Study 1**

*Reading: John 13:33—14:6*

1. Study the conversation in verses 33-38. Note the questions and the answers. Why do you think Peter failed to hear Jesus give the new commandment in verses 34 and 35? What evidence do you see that Peter needed to hear those words?
2. What encouragement can you draw from Peter's experience?
3. In verse 34 we are commanded to love others as Jesus loved the disciples. Specifically, how can you translate that command into your own life?
4. What can you learn about the "place" from Jesus' words in 14:1-4?
5. Note Thomas' question and Jesus' reply in verses 5 and 6. What, exactly, do Jesus' words mean to you? Read Acts 4:12 for additional understanding.

☐ **Study 2**

*Reading: John 14:7-15*

1. In verses 7-11 Jesus and Philip seem to be thinking on two different levels. What do you think Philip understood "knowing" the Father and "knowing" Jesus to mean? What did the term "knowing" mean to Jesus as you understand his definition from these verses?
2. From your study of verses 7-11, what do you believe is essential before you can "know" God the Father?
3. List some of the things Jesus has been doing as you have observed them in the book of John. What evidence do you see in our world today that the words of Jesus in verse 12 are true?
4. In verse 13, what do you think asking "in the name" of Jesus really means?
5. What relationship do you see between verses 12-14 and verse 15?

☐ **Study 3**

*Reading: John 14:16-31*

1. What are some of the things you can learn about the interrelationship of the Father, Son, and Holy Spirit from a study of verses 16-24?
2. In verses 21-24 Jesus gives the test for those who love him. And he states the rewards. How would you evaluate this exchange of love between God and man?
3. In verses 16, 17, 25, and 26, Jesus speaks of "another Counselor," the "Spirit of Truth," the "Holy Spirit." What evidence do you have from these verses that the titles are descriptive of the Spirit's work within the believer?
4. What experience have you had with the peace of God explained in verse 27?
5. What indications does Jesus give in verses 28-31 that the disciples have not yet understood either his love or his peace?

☐ **Study 4**

*Reading: John 15:1-17*

1. Study verses 1-6 to get a clear picture of the work of the Father, the Son, and the believer. What help for the believer is suggested

in verse 3 and again in 1 John 2:24?

2. What kinds of "fruit" do you think a believer is expected to produce through remaining in Christ?
3. Study the positive conditions and the results which occur in verses 5, 7, 10, and 16 below:

| *Condition* | *Result* |
|---|---|
| If a man remains in me and I in him, | he will bear much fruit; |
| If you remain in me and my words remain in you, | ask whatever you wish, and it will be given you. |
| If you obey my commands, | you will remain in my love. . . . |
| Go and bear fruit—fruit that will last. | Then the Father will give you whatever you ask in my name. |

What can you learn from this study? Now look at the negative condition and result in verse 6. What does this add to your understanding of Jesus' requirements for the believer?

4. By examining verses 9-17, what can you find out about the kind of love Jesus commands us to have for each other? Think of two people you know who come closest to having this kind of love. How do you think they are able to love in this way?

### □ Study 5

*Reading: 1 John 3:11-24*

1. Compare the teachings of Jesus in John 15:9-19 with the words of his disciple, John, in 1 John 3:11-18. The Master had spoken the words recorded in the Gospel and been put to death more than half a century before the disciple wrote his words in the letter. How do you feel about John's understanding of Jesus' teachings on love?
2. What evidence can you find in verses 16-22 that John is calling for a love of action toward our brothers and toward God?
3. In what ways have you tested the truth of John's statements in verses 23 and 24? What is required of us according to these verses?

## Lesson 7 Overview

1. Look back over Lesson 7 to discover some of the ways in which the disciples learned to love. By what methods are you learning to love?

2. What are some of the things you learned from this lesson about the Holy Spirit? In what ways can he help you to obey Jesus' command to love others?

3. What fruit has been produced in your life through the work of the Holy Spirit in your heart this week?

4. Reread any unanswered questions remaining from previous lessons. Can you now answer them? Write down any new questions arising from your study of Lesson 7. Watch for answers as you continue your study.

# EIGHT
# Jesus: The Spirit of Truth

*John 15:18—16:33; 1 John 4:1-6*

*Truthful Spirit, dwell with me;*
*I myself would truthful be;*
*And with wisdom kind and clear*
*Let Thy life in mine appear;*
*And with actions brotherly*
*Speak my Lord's sincerity.*

Thomas Toke Lynch
("Gracious Spirit, Dwell with Me")

☐ **Study 1**

*Reading: John 15:18—16:4*

1. In what ways was Lesson 7 a preparation for this reading in John 15:18—16:4?
2. In this reading the world is clearly identified with hatred—not love. Why do you think "belonging to the world" generates hatred of Jesus Christ?
3. Jesus warns that believers will be rejected and persecuted. "No servant," he says, "is greater than his master." What forms have rejection and persecution taken in your life?

□ **Study 2**

*Reading: John 16:5-15*

1. Why do you think the disciples did not ask Jesus where he was going? (verse 5). What has occurred since Peter asked the question (13:36) and Thomas asked the question (14:5) to cause such silence now?
2. Study verse 7 carefully. Note the ways in which Jesus emphasizes his point. Why do you think it was so important that the disciples understand this truth? Why is it important that we understand it today?
3. What evidence do you see in verses 8-11 that the Holy Spirit is to be an active force in the lives of unbelievers?
4. From verses 13-15 list the work Jesus says the Holy Spirit is to perform in the lives of believers.
5. From your own experience and observation, what evidence can you give that the Holy Spirit is still at work in these same ways today? (See verses 8-15.)

□ **Study 3**

*Reading: John 16:16-24*

1. Judging by the questions in verses 17-19, what parts of Jesus' teachings in verses 5-16 do you think the disciples have been able to grasp?
2. What words in verses 20-22 are contrasted with the word "joy"? Why do you think Jesus' analogy in verse 21 is a good one to illustrate what he was teaching the disciples?
3. What do you understand to be the causes of this joy the disciples are promised? Do you experience this same joy today?
4. What can you learn about prayer from a close study of verses 23 and 24?

□ **Study 4**

*Reading: John 16:25-33*

1. In verse 25 Jesus points ahead by saying "a time is coming." In verse 26 he refers to "that day." From evidence within these two verses, what period in time do you think Jesus was referring to?
2. In what way do verses 26 and 27 add to your understanding of

what Jesus means by the words "ask in my name"?

3. Note the descending/ascending order in verse 28. What significance does this have for you?
4. Study verses 29-33. What three words would you use to describe the disciples at this time? What three words would you use to describe Jesus as you see him in these verses?
5. How do you think we can have "peace" and "trouble" at the same time? What examples from your experience can support your answer?

□ **Study 5**

*Reading: 1 John 4:1-6*

1. This reading is clearly a contrast of two sides headed by the Spirit of God and the spirit of antichrist. Make two columns and divide the points given about each side. How can these lists be useful to you today?
2. What additional information can you add to these two lists from studying the words of Jesus in John 8:42-47?
3. What evidence do you see in our world today that false teaching is enjoying some degree of success? What should be the attitude toward this success on the part of those who believe in Jesus Christ?
4. Reread verses 1-6 and write down the ideas which give you confidence and make you feel secure as a believer in Jesus Christ.

## Lesson 8 Overview

1. What are some of the reasons why people choose to follow the world rather than follow Jesus Christ? Why do those who follow the world often persecute those who believe in Jesus Christ?

2. What did Jesus teach that the work of the Holy Spirit would be?

3. How can we test the spirits as we are commanded to do in 1 John 4:1?

4. Check any unanswered questions from previous lessons. Did you find answers? Write down any questions still unanswered after Lesson 8, and watch for answers as you continue your study.

# NINE

# Jesus: Perfect Love

*John 17:1—18:27; 1 John 4:7-21*

*Love divine, all loves excelling,*
*Joy of heav'n, to earth come down;*
*Fix in us thy humble dwelling;*
*All thy faithful mercies crown.*
*Jesus, thou art all compassion,*
*Pure, unbounded love thou art;*
*Visit us with thy salvation;*
*Enter every trembling heart.*

Charles Wesley

☐ **Study 1**

*Reading: John 17:1-19*

1. What can you learn about God and about the significance of Jesus' words "the time has come" (verse 1) by tracing the phrase through the following verses: 2:4; 7:6, 30; 8:20; 13:1; 17:1?
2. In verses 1-5 Jesus prays for himself. What can you say about "glory" and "glorify" from evidence found in these verses?
3. In verses 6-9 Jesus introduces his prayer for the disciples who are with him. List the verbs which tell what Jesus has done for them. List the verbs which tell how they have responded to Jesus and

his words. What can you learn from this?

4. In verses 10-19 Jesus continues his prayer for his disciples. Write down the things Jesus asks the Father to do for them. Why are these requests sufficient for the disciples' needs?

☐ **Study 2**

*Reading: John 17:20-26*

1. In verses 20-26 Jesus prays for all future believers. In what ways do you see his desires for the body of believers being answered today? What parts of his prayer are yet to be fulfilled?
2. What can you learn about the love of God from your observation of the relationship between the Father and the Son in these verses?
3. What evidence do you find in these verses that Jesus loves you?

☐ **Study 3**

*Reading: John 18:1-14*

1. In what way does the theme of darkness and light set the tone of these verses? (Note specifically verses 2 and 3.)
2. Study the words of Jesus in verses 4-10 and the reaction of those who came to arrest him. What significance do you see in this exchange?
3. Note the metaphor of the "cup" used by Jesus in verse 11. Now read Isaiah 51:17 and Jeremiah 25:17 in which the metaphor is used in a similar way. How do the Old Testament references help you to understand Jesus' reference to drinking the "cup" in John 18:11? How do you explain Mark 10:38, 39 in relation to this verse?

☐ **Study 4**

*Reading: John 18:15-27*

1. In what ways is the character of Peter revealed in John 18:10 consistent or inconsistent with his actions in verses 15-18 and 25-27?
2. What two words best describe the character of Jesus as revealed by his words in verses 19-24? How do you think Peter could deny such a Master?
3. Can you recall a situation in which you, like Peter, denied Jesus Christ? What do you think caused your denial?

□ **Study 5**

*Reading: 1 John 4:7-21*

1. How would you define "love," from what we are told in these verses about God's way of loving us?
2. What evidence can you find in this reading to support the statement that if the Spirit of God lives within us, we have his perfect love within us?
3. In what ways does John say our love for God is manifest?
4. What kinds of things do we fear that keep us from loving others as Jesus does? How is this fear a denial of Jesus?
5. Read Romans 14:10-13 and Galatians 6:7-10. What do these verses add to John's teachings about love?

## Lesson 9 Overview

1. Go back to the Lesson 4 overview and see how you answered the questions on love. What new things have you learned about love from Lesson 9?

2. Do you think we sometimes deny Jesus because we want to go the selfish ways of the world more than we want to follow Jesus' perfect example of love?

3. Are there any questions still unanswered from previous lessons? Write down any new questions you have after studying Lesson 9. Watch for answers as you continue your study.

# TEN

# The New Birth: Victory in Christ

*John 18:28—20:10; 1 John 5:1-12*

*Was it for crimes that I had done,*
*He groaned upon the tree?*
*Amazing pity! grace unknown!*
*And love beyond degree!*

Isaac Watts
("At the Cross")

☐ **Study 1**

*Reading: John 18:28—19:16*

1. Do a close study of Pilate in this reading. Examine his words, his actions, his choices. Trace Pilate's wavering decisions leading to his choice in 19:16: "Finally Pilate handed him over to them to be crucified." In what ways do you identify with Pilate?
2. What evidence do you see in this reading that a fair trial before the Sanhedrin is not a possibility?
3. Why do you think Jesus did not answer Pilate's question, "What is truth?" in 18:38?
4. In what way is Barabbas' release a symbol of the effects of substitutionary atonement? What does this have to do with you?

☐ **Study 2**

*Reading: John 19:17-27*

1. What evidence do you see in verses 19-22 that Pilate knew who Jesus was but chose to reject him?
2. Do you think the guilt of the chief priests is any greater or less than that of the soldiers (verses 17-24)? Is their guilt greater than that of Barabbas? Do you think the guilt of any of these men is greater than yours?
3. What can you learn from verses 25-27 about Jesus? about responsibilities of sons? about responsibilities of a disciple of Jesus Christ?

☐ **Study 3**

*Reading: John 19:28-42*

1. Explain what you believe Jesus meant when he said, "It is finished" (verse 30).
2. In verses 28, 36, and 37, reference is made to Scriptures being fulfilled. Look up Psalm 69:21; Exodus 12:46; Psalm 34:20; and Zechariah 12:10 and compare these verses to John 19:28-37. What do you learn about God from this?
3. What is your reaction to Joseph of Arimathea and to Nicodemus in verses 38-42? In what ways can you identify with one or both of them?

☐ **Study 4**

*Reading: John 20:1-10*

1. Think back over past lessons. What preparation had Jesus given his disciples for his resurrection? Why do you suppose they were so surprised to find an empty tomb?
2. What do you think the "other disciple" of verse 8 "saw and believed"?
3. Note the details John uses to tell this story. Why would John feel such exact reporting was important?
4. What does Jesus' resurrection mean to you?

☐ **Study 5**

*Reading: 1 John 5:1-12*

1. What do you think the term "born of God" in verse 1 means? Is this what we mean when we speak of being "born again"—a term we hear often today?
2. What results of believing that Jesus is the Christ can you find in verses 1-5?
3. What are some possible meanings for the "water" and the "blood" in verses 6-8? In what ways have the water and blood become symbolized for us today?
4. How does the Spirit testify to us? What is the testimony? (See verses 9-12.)
5. On a scale of 1-10 how would you rate your assurance that you have victory over death and the gift of eternal life in Christ Jesus?

### Lesson 10 Overview

1. After studying this lesson, how would you explain Romans 6:23 to a friend?

2. What additional understanding has this lesson given to John 5:24?

3. What is your reaction to Isaac Watts' words printed at the beginning of this lesson?

4. Are there any questions still unanswered from previous lessons? Write down any new questions you have from Lesson 10 and watch for answers as you continue your study.

# ELEVEN

# Jesus: Our Way, Our Truth, Our Life

*John 20:11—21:25; 1 John 5:13-21*

*"But as for me, I know that my Redeemer lives, and that he will stand upon the earth at last. And I know that after this body has decayed, this body shall see God!"*

Job 19:25, 26 (TLB)

☐ **Study 1**

*Reading: John 20:11-23*

1. List all the facts given about the angels in verses 11-13. What significance can these facts have for us today?
2. What are some of the reasons why you think Jesus appeared to Mary of Magdala before anyone else? What qualified her to meet Jesus? (See verses 11-18. Also look back at 20:1.)
3. What evidence do you find in verses 19-23 that the purpose of Jesus' mission to earth did not change after his resurrection?
4. Recall other times in John's Gospel when Jesus banished fear with his peace. What proof do you have in your own life that fear can be banished by the peace of Jesus?

□ **Study 2**

*Reading: John 20:24-31*

1. Trace Thomas' road to belief by a close study of John 11:16; 14:5-7; and 20:24-29. In what ways does Thomas' journey resemble your own?
2. What can you learn about the disciples from a study of verses 19 and 26 in this chapter?
3. Why do you think Jesus continued to do "many other miraculous signs" (verse 30) after he was resurrected?
4. In what specific ways are the "miraculous signs" which John records in verses 24-29 an aid to your belief that "Jesus is the Christ, the Son of God" (verse 31)?

□ **Study 3**

*Reading: John 21:1-14*

1. In what ways is the setting for the disciples (Sea of Tiberias) and the setting for Jesus (on the shore) important to the full understanding of verses 1-7?
2. John, the author and disciple, often refers to himself as "the disciple whom Jesus loved" (verse 7). Study the actions of Peter and John in John 20:3-8 and John 21:7, 8. What do these actions reveal about their characters?
3. Why do you think Jesus fed the disciples again? (See verses 9-13.)
4. Do you see anything unusual in the author's comments about the disciples in verse 12? What do these statements have to do with Jesus' words which precede them and his actions which follow them?

□ **Study 4**

*Reading: John 21:15-25*

1. This is the third time Jesus has appeared to the disciples following his resurrection. Go back and reread John 20:19-23 and 26-29, imagining that you are Peter on these occasions. Now follow Peter through this third appearance of Jesus to the disciples. What do you think Peter has been thinking and feeling prior to the time Jesus addresses him in verse 15?
2. What relationship do you see between Peter's denial of Jesus as

recorded in John 18:15-27 and Jesus' conversation with Peter as recorded in John 21:15-19?

3. Study the three questions, three answers, and three commands which appear in the conversation between Jesus and Peter (verses 15-19). What do you think Peter learned from this? What can all disciples of Jesus Christ learn from this?
4. What are some of the lessons you can learn from verses 20-23 about your relationship to Jesus and to other Christians?
5. What thoughts do you have after reading verses 24 and 25?

☐ **Study 5**

*Reading: 1 John 5:13-21*

1. Note again in verse 13 John's purpose in writing this letter. What difference does it make in a person when he *knows* he has eternal life?
2. What can you learn about prayer from a careful study of verses 14 and 15?
3. Why do you think John enclosed the comments on prayer, found in verses 14 and 15, between his comments on eternal life found in verses 13 and 16?
4. What is your understanding of a "sin that leads to death" which John refers to in verses 16 and 17?
5. List all of the things that "we know" recorded by John in verses 18-20. On a scale of 1-10 how would you rate your assurance of each of these?
6. John's final warning is, "Keep yourselves from idols." What kinds of things are idols today? Are any of these temptations a problem for you?

## Lesson 11 Overview

1. What evidence do you find in this lesson that Jesus Christ did, indeed, rise from the dead as he said he would?

2. Let's look at the founders of the four major world religions. Abraham, the father of Judaism, died about 1900 B.C. Followers of Buddha claim that after his death nothing whatever remained behind. Mohammed died in A.D. 632 and devout Mohammedans annually visit his tomb in Medina. Only Christianity claims an

empty tomb and a resurrection for its founder. In what ways are these unique claims of Christianity essential to our belief that Jesus Christ is our Way, our Truth, and our Life?

*Discussion Leader's Guide*

# ONE

# Jesus: The Word of Life

*John 1—3; 1 John 1:1-4*

## Objectives

1. To understand John's purposes in writing both John and 1 John.
2. To take note of the words and phrases John uses and grapple with their deeper meanings.
3. To see Jesus, flesh and spirit, man and God, the Word of life.

## Background Information

In Greek philosophy the term *logos* which translates into English as "word" was well known to represent the logical nature of man. In a broader sense it represented the principle which governed the order of the material world.

A philosophy called gnosticism, prevalent in early Christian times, held that the material world was evil and the spiritual world good. Those gnostics who tried to hold onto this belief while moving into the Christian faith reasoned that the Spirit entered Jesus, the man, at his baptism, but departed from him prior to his death. The bridge to God, they felt, was not through a divine Savior who died for their sins, but through their own superior knowledge, gleaned from much study. The intellect was admired; the body was of no value.

No doubt John was very much aware of this false teaching filtering into the church when he wrote his Gospel and 1 John. And had he done nothing more than combat the teaching of gnosticism, his words would have had great value. But he did far more.

The use of the term "word" was not new to biblical writings. John draws heavily on the Old Testament concept of the word—God's word—active and moving in our world. In the very beginning God created the heaven and the earth by his word. "God said . . . . And it was so."

Joseph Parker, writing more than a hundred years ago *(The People's Bible,* I, 103), described this action of God's word as we see it in the creation story of Genesis 1, 2:

*The action never pauses for a moment; how busy are the days, and how active the night in star-lighting; in the waters is a great stir of life; the woods are burning with colour; the earth is alive with things that creep; the air vibrates with the clap of wings.*

God's word was active not only in creating but in healing (Psalm 107:20), in speaking to the prophets (Jeremiah 1:11, 13), bringing visions (Ezekiel 1:1-3), and judging (Joel 1). In Isaiah 45:23, God declares, "My mouth has uttered in all integrity a word that will not be revoked."

God is personified in his word. His word has power and authority, and it will accomplish what he sends it forth to accomplish (Isaiah 55:11).

But we get even more than personification when we read in John's Gospel, "In the beginning was the Word, and the Word was with God, and the Word was God." We see a relationship: an intimate, personal relationship of the Word to God. The Word was not created; the Word was God. Then John goes on to say, "The Word became flesh and lived for a while among us. We have seen his glory, the glory of the one and only Son, who came from the Father, full of grace and truth" (John 1:14). Now we get a sense of the intimate, personal relationship God desires to have with us. This is what John wants us to believe and to know.

After chapter 1 in John and verse 1 of 1 John, the term "the Word" is not used again in a personal sense. Instead, the Word appears as the very *life* of mankind and as the *light* of the world.

### Visual Aid

With a heavy marker pen, print the words of John 1:1 on poster paper or brown wrapping paper.

*In the beginning was the Word*
*and the Word was with God,*
*and the Word was God.*

John 1:1

Tape this visual aid to the wall above the name tag table, or in some other prominent place in the room. This will tend to focus the thinking of the group on the theme of the lesson from the beginning. You may wish to refer to the verse during and at the end of the study as well.

# TWO
# Jesus: The Light in Fellowship

*John 4—5; 1 John 1:5-10*

## Objectives

1. To understand the symbolism of light and darkness.
2. To see the clear division between God's kingdom and Satan's kingdom.
3. To realize that the words of Jesus are true and can lead us from darkness into the light of his fellowship.

## Background Information

*Symbols of light and darkness:* John, perhaps more than any other writer in the Bible, uses figurative language to heighten and enhance the meaning of words. This does not mean that we are not to read his stories literally. Indeed, symbolism rests on things which have great literal importance. But it does mean that if we are to understand the deeper meaning of John's words, we must give thought to symbolic truths as well.

In Lesson 2, light and darkness are strong symbols. In Scripture, these symbols appear often. For example, Exodus 10:21-23 tells us that one of the plagues God sent on the Egyptians was deep darkness, while the Israelites had light as usual. We may read this literally (it really happened) and symbolically (the Egyptians rejected God; the Israelites believed God).

David said, "My God turns my darkness into light" (Psalm 18:28), and Isaiah wrote, "The people walking in darkness have seen a great light; on those living in the land of the shadow of death a light has dawned" (Isaiah 9:2).

Clearly the symbol of light refers to our Lord and his kingdom (1 John 1:5), while the symbol of darkness refers to Satan and his kingdom (Ephesians 6:12). When the light (Jesus Christ and his truth) penetrates our darkness (the sin and rejection in our minds), we begin to move into God's kingdom. Peter wrote, "You may declare the praises of him who called you out of darkness into his wonderful light" (1 Peter 2:9).

The Samaritan woman is a good example of one who lived in mental darkness. She did not know the truth. As Jesus began to teach her, and she began to understand more and more truth, light dispelled her darkness.

The nobleman, a royal official, lived in darkness. He asked for a physical healing for his son, but got far more. He and his household were led by Jesus from the dark kingdom of Satan into God's kingdom of light.

You may wish to explore the following Scripture verses which are a sampling of many which use the light/darkness symbol: Psalm 18:28; 107:10-14; 112:4; Proverbs 4:18, 19; Micah 7:8; 2 Cor. 6:14; Ephesians 5:8.

*Signs and works:* John sees the seven miracles he records in his Gospel as parables or "signs" of the power and authority of Jesus Christ. Each of the miracles teaches truth, reveals who Jesus is, and points the way to God—the way out of darkness into light. One of the miracles occurred in Lesson 1: the changing of water into wine (John 2:1-11); two occur in Lesson 2: the healing of the nobleman's son (John 4:46-54) and the healing at the pool (John 5:1-15). Watch for the remaining four: in Lesson 3: the feeding of the 5,000 (John 6:1-14), and Jesus walking on the water (John 6:16-21); in Lesson 5: the healing of the blind man (John 9:1-41), and the raising of Lazarus (John 11:1-46).

## Visual Aids

1. If you are teaching at night, turn off the lights and light a candle. Point out that the light from the candle banishes the darkness close to it. The closer you come to the candle, the more light you have. The closer we come to Jesus, the more understanding we have of his truths. Sometimes, like the Samaritan woman, our move from darkness to light is gradual.

2. Using a chalkboard or poster paper, make two columns: one headed "Darkness," the other "Light." Have members of the group contribute truths learned about each from today's lesson and from reading the following: Psalm 27:1; 43:3; 119:105; Proverbs 4:19; Isaiah 5:20; Micah 7:9; Matthew 4:16; Luke 1:79; John 3:19; Ephesians 6:12; 1 Peter 2:9; and 1 John 1:5.

Encourage members to watch for further truths about darkness and light as they continue their study of John and 1 John.

# THREE
# Jesus: Our Advocate

*John 6—7:24; 1 John 2:1-6*

## Objectives

1. To understand how Jesus, at the time of the Passover Feast, used the symbols of bread, flesh, and blood ("hard teaching") to help men to see their need for a savior and an advocate before the Father.
2. To realize how much God desires that we do not sin.
3. To see the love of God in providing for us an advocate, his Son Jesus Christ, when we do sin.

## Background Information

*Passover:* Read about the Passover Feast in Exodus 12, Deuteronomy 16:1-8, and Hebrews 11:28. The word "Passover" comes from the Hebrew *pesah*, meaning "to spare." In New Testament times the Passover Feast celebrated not only God's sparing from the death penalty the firstborn son in families who trusted him, but also the saving of Israelites from lives of slavery to the Egyptians. In addition, the blood of the lamb that was ceremonially killed by the priest in the Temple was poured on the altar as an offering for sin. To take part in the Passover Feast, a participant had to eat the unleavened bread and the flesh of the lamb—both prepared in special ways for the occasion.

The Passover Feast, then, was a time to remember God's salvation of his people and to receive his forgiveness for sin.

In John 6:1-15, at the time of the Passover, Jesus himself supplied the feast and fed 5,000 people. Later (verse 35) he taught, "I am the bread of life." He referred back to the Father's feeding of their forefathers in the desert and pointed forward to his becoming not only their bread of life but their sacrificial Passover lamb (verses 48-59).

Ultimately the early Christians understood this and the Passover Feast became our Lord's Supper or Communion Service.

*Atonement:* Jesus Christ is called the "atoning sacrifice for our sins" in 1 John 2:2. This makes it possible for him to be our advocate before the Father. The Old Testament as well as the New teaches that all men are sinners and are separated from God because of sin. (See 1 Kings 8:46; Ecclesiastes 7:20; Isaiah 59:2; and Romans 3:23.) Death is recognized as the penalty for sin (Ezekiel 18:20), bringing about total separation from God.

But God instituted the substitutionary sacrifice for man's sins. He explained the necessity of shedding blood, in Leviticus 17:11. "For the life of a creature is in the blood, and I have given it to you to make atonement for yourselves on the altar; it is the blood that makes atonement for one's life." The author of Hebrews 9:22 later wrote, "Without the shedding of blood there is no forgiveness."

The Old Testament sacrifices are a foreshadowing of the supreme and final atonement of the Son of God for our sins. John the Baptist announced the coming of Christ by shouting, "Look, the Lamb of God, who takes away the sin of the world!" (John 1:29). Paul writes in 1 Corinthians 5:7, "For Christ, our Passover lamb, has been sacrificed."

The atonement for our sins proceeds from the very heart of God. It is a heart of pure love. Remember John 3:16? "For God so loved the world that he gave his one and only Son, that whoever believes in him shall not perish but have eternal life."

## Visual Aids

1. Print 1 John 1:9 on poster paper and place it in a prominent place in the room. You may wish to refer to the verse to close the discussion. This will emphasize not only God's love in providing an atoning sacrifice for our sins through his Son, but also his love in continually forgiving us when we confess our sins.

2. In the event someone does not know Jesus as Savior, or some Christian is unsure, have some literature available to take home. Most denominations have booklets explaining how to become a Christian. Or Inter-Varsity Christian Fellowship's *Becoming a Christian* or Campus Crusade's *Four Spiritual Laws* may be used.

# FOUR

# Love: The New Commandment

*John 7:25—8:59; 1 John 2:7-17*

## Objectives

1. To see Jesus' steadfast love as it is demonstrated again and again, regardless of opposition, persecution, and rejection.
2. To grasp what Jesus meant when he commanded us to love others as he loves us.
3. To understand God's love for those in his family—children who walk in light; and his concern for those who cling to the world—children who walk in darkness.

## Background Information

*Jesus as the Christ:* The word "Christ" is the Greek equivalent for the Hebrew word "Messiah" meaning "anointed one." There is ample evidence in the Old Testament that the Jews expected God to intervene again in history by sending a messiah who would judge the world, destroy evil, and deliver the Jews from the domination of other nations. This messiah would be a conquering hero who would set up God's kingdom of righteousness on earth. With their minds rooted in the world, many Jews had difficulty seeing their need for a messiah who came to be their sacrificial, Passover lamb, their only way to eternal life.

*Adultery:* One of the Ten Commandments, Exodus 20:14, says, "You shall not commit adultery." Leviticus 20:10 gives the penalty for breaking the commandment: death to both the man and woman. Job 24:15-17 describes an adulterer as one who "watches for the dusk" and "keeps his faith concealed." He makes "friends with the terrors of darkness."

The teachers of the law and the Pharisees who brought the woman caught in adultery to Jesus in the Temple court certainly knew the seriousness of the sin. Jesus knew too. (See Matthew 5:27-32.) But Jesus also knew the judgmental, self-righteous attitude of these men. (Remember the parable Jesus told about the Pharisee who prayed on the street corner: "God, I thank you that I am not like all other men—robbers, evildoers, adulterers . . ." Luke 18:11). The accusers had broken the greater law: they did not love.

In Romans 13:9, 10 Paul explained that the commandments not to commit adultery, murder, to steal or covet, are summed up in one rule: "Love your neighbor as yourself" because "love does no harm to its neighbor. Therefore love is the fulfillment of the law."

Jesus loved the woman caught in adultery. He recognized her sin, but he did not condemn her. Rather he said, "Go and sin no more."

*Family of God:* The "family of God" theme comes together with the theme of "darkness and light" in this lesson. So far John has taught that "God is light, and in him is no darkness at all." Children of God obey his commands and, therefore, walk in his light. Now 1 John 2:7-17 deals with relationships within God's family. To be in God's family we must love each other. The words addressed to children, fathers, and young men have been interpreted to mean various stages of growth in the Christian life. But these words can also help us to see what has happened to those who have moved from darkness into light—from the family of the evil one into the family of God.

### Visual Aids

Print the personalized paraphrase of John 13:34, 35 on small cards, inserting the name of the receiver. Distribute these at the close of the class session. For example:

*Jane, I am giving a new commandment to you now—love others just as much as I love you. Your strong love for others will prove to the world that you are my disciple.*

# FIVE

# God's Children: Their Choices and Dangers

*John 9—11:46; 1 John 2:18-29*

## Objectives

1. To study the characters in these stories in their crises as Jesus caused them to make choices.
2. To examine the dangers faced by those in the stories who made the wrong choices.
3. To understand the choices imposed on every man by Jesus Christ and the dangers imposed on every man by antichrists.

## Background Information

*Sin:* The biblical view of sin is that it is always directed against God. It is the contradiction of God's perfection. Paul said, "The sinful mind is hostile to God" (Romans 8:7); and John wrote, "Everyone who sins breaks the law; in fact, sin is lawlessness" (1 John 3:4). Sin begins in the mind and heart. Satan reached Eve when he suggested a way in which she could become as wise as God. She made her choice inwardly, and then she acted upon her choice. Just as Eve chose to oppose God's law, to disobey him, so man today chooses to sin. Perhaps, then, we can define sin as a conscious choice which man makes to oppose God, his laws, and his plans.

*Antichrist:* The term "antichrist" is found only in the works of John, but teaching about it is widespread in the Bible. In 1 John 2:18 the author states, "You have heard that the antichrist is coming, even now many antichrists have come." The one evil personality John refers to is explained more fully in Revelation as the one who will come at the end of the age. But the "many antichrists" are all those who deny "that Jesus is the Christ" (1 John 2:22). This denial is in direct opposition to the work of God and to his plan of salvation for man. To become antichrist involves an attitude and a heart choice—a choice to oppose Christ and to align with the side of Satan.

*Feast of Dedication (or Feast of Lights, or Hanukkah):* This eight-day feast, celebrated on the twenty-fifth day of the Hebrew month Cheslev, is a commemoration of a victory won by a priest named Mattathias and his followers against a Syrian army. In 167 B.C. the Temple at Jerusalem was desecrated by a forced sacrifice to Zeus. Mattathias and his sons quickly gathered an army, fought the Syrians, and forced them to repeal their laws against worship of the one true God.

Observance of the Feast of Dedication is, even today, marked by the lighting of eight candles—one on each day of the feast. Jesus had repeatedly declared, "I am the light of the world," yet the Jews who gathered around him at this feast in Jerusalem walked in darkness.

## Visual Aids

1. Lesson 5 includes the last of the seven "signs" of the power and authority of Jesus Christ. List the signs on a chart and, with the group, trace the buildup of evidence through these signs that Jesus is indeed the Son of God.

*Signs of the Power and Authority of Jesus Christ*

1. John 2:1-11. Changing water into wine.
2. John 4:46-54. Healing of nobleman's son.
3. John 5:1-15. Healing of man at pool.

4. John 6:1-14. Feeding of the 5,000.
5. John 6:16-21. Jesus walking on water.
6. John 9:1-12. Healing of blind man.
7. John 11:1-46. Raising of Lazarus.

2. Discuss more fully what it means to hold fast to the truths of Christ and to recognize our position as believers in the Son and the Father. Print the following words from today's lesson, 1 John 2:24, 27, on poster paper, and use them as your guide for discussion.

*1 John 2:24, 27*
See that what you have heard
from the beginning *remains in you.*
If it does, you will also *remain in the Son*
*and in the Father.*
As for you, the anointing you
received from him *remains in you . . .*
*remain in him.*

# SIX

# God's Children: Striving for Obedience

*John 11:47—13:32; 1 John 3:1-10*

### Objectives

1. To examine the obedience of those who surrounded Jesus during the last week of his ministry on earth.
2. To observe the full extent of obedience as it was taught and demonstrated by our Lord Jesus.
3. To test our own willingness to live our lives in obedience to Jesus Christ.

### Background Information

*The Passover and Jesus Christ, the Lamb of God:* John specifically notes three Passovers in his Gospel: John 2:13; 6:4; and 11:55. Each time he refers to the feast as the "Jewish Passover." In John 5:1, reference is made to a "feast of the Jews" which is generally believed to be a fourth Passover.

While Jesus went to Jerusalem for the celebration of these feasts, the last one recorded in John 11:55 marked the close of his ministry on earth. Jesus knew that simultaneous with the Jewish sacrifice of their Passover lambs, he would become God's sacrifice—the final sacrifice—for the sins of the world.

The Lord's Supper, commemorating Jesus' sacrifice, would replace the Jewish Passover Feast. The memorial offering of the Passover bread and cup that Jesus shared with his disciples on Thursday night of that last week is not recorded by John, but the other three Gospels include it (Matthew 26:26-30; Mark 14:22-26; and Luke 22:19, 20).

*Sanhedrin:* The Jerusalem Sanhedrin was the high council of Judaism. Headed by the high priest, Caiaphas, at the time of Jesus' arrest, the Sanhedrin was composed of seventy men, the majority of whom were Pharisees. Some were priests and scribes; others were wealthy men such as Nicodemus and Joseph of Arimathea, who were probably landowners.

The powers of the Sanhedrin were extensive; however, its direct powers were limited to Judea during the time of Christ. Exercising both civil and criminal jurisdiction over Jewish people, the Sanhedrin could order arrests and judge all cases which did not involve capital punishment. Death sentences had to be confirmed by the Roman procurator.

Pilate was the procurator during Jesus' last days on earth. At this time the Sanhedrin was dominated by Pharisees since Herod the Great had killed forty-five of the Sadducee members in 37 B.C. The Sadducee party never did regain control.

## Visual Aids

1. Have a small table in the room spread with a white cloth. On the table place bread and wine (or grape juice) to remind members of the group of the Last Supper Jesus had with his disciples, and which he calls us to share.

2. Would you dare to wash each others' feet as Jesus did? Reread John 13:13-17. If your group is meeting at a time when this is possible, it will be an unforgettable experience.

3. As a group you may wish to look up the references to Old Testament prophecy which occur in this lesson. Print them on poster paper:

| *New Testament* | from | *Old Testament* |
|---|---|---|
| John 12:13 | | Psalm 118:25, 26 |
| John 12:15 | | Zechariah 9:9 |
| John 12:38 | | Isaiah 53:1 |
| John 12:40 | | Isaiah 6:10 |

# SEVEN

# God's Children: Learning to Love

*John 13:33—15:17; 1 John 3:11-24*

## Objectives

1. To explore what knowing God and loving him really mean.
2. To study Jesus' command to love others as he loved us and determine ways in which that command should be carried out in our lives.
3. To see the need for the Holy Spirit in our lives if we are to love and obey God.

## Background Information

*Holy Spirit:* In this lesson, Jesus promised to send the Holy Spirit to "teach you all things" and "remind you of everything I have said to you" (John 14:26). In Lesson 8 more is taught about the work of the Holy Spirit. As a discussion leader you will want to be prepared to help the group understand the work of the Holy Spirit—essential if we are to love and obey Jesus Christ. Books about the Holy Spirit listed in your Suggested Study References at the back of this book will help you. The following outline is given for your Bible study and possible presentation to your group:

Who is the Holy Spirit?

1. He is the Spirit of God, the third person of the Trinity. *Genesis 1:2.*

2. Before Jesus came, the Holy Spirit rested upon men who were called to do specific tasks—prophets or kings. Examples: *Isaiah 61:1; Psalm 51:11.*

3. After his resurrection, Jesus appeared to 120 people in an upper room in Jerusalem and promised that they all would receive the Holy Spirit. *Acts 1:3-9.*

4. This happened on the day of Pentecost. *Acts 2:1-4.*

5. The promise of the Holy Spirit is for all believers. *Acts 2:38, 39.*

Why do we need the Holy Spirit?

1. He glorifies God and guides us into truth. *John 16:13, 14.*

2. He teaches us. *John 14:26.*

3. He leads us. *Romans 8:14.*

4. He intercedes for us. *Romans 8:26.*

5. He develops our characters. *Galatians 5:22-25.*

6. He gives us gifts for the good of Christ's body of believers. *1 Corinthians 12:1-7.*

7. He is God's power working in and through us. *John 15:5.*

How may we be filled with the Holy Spirit?

1. We simply ask. *Luke 11:9-13.*

2. Remember: We are commanded to be filled with his Spirit. *Ephesians 5:18.*

The Holy Spirit is a wonderful gift of God; his Spirit within us helps us to obey God's commands, to love others as he loves us.

## Visual Aids

1. Print the following great "I am" statements of Jesus on poster paper:

| | |
|---|---|
| *John 6:35:* | I am the bread of life. |
| *John 8:12:* | I am the light of the world. |
| *John 10:9:* | I am the door. |
| *John 10:11:* | I am the good shepherd. |
| *John 11:25:* | I am the resurrection and the life. |
| *John 14:6:* | I am the way, the truth and the life. |
| *John 15:1:* | I am the true vine. |

Ask seven members of the group to read the verses from their Bibles. As each verse is read, discuss the work of Jesus' ministry which it illustrates. Each "I am" statement explains something Jesus came to do for us. Should it not be easy for us to love and obey one who loves us so much?

2. Have a number of books on the Holy Spirit available for group members to take home and study. Your pastor may recommend some. Suggestions: Campus Crusade's booklet, *Have You Made the Wonderful Discovery of the Spirit-Filled Life?* is available in Bible bookstores for 10¢. Excellent paperbacks are *The Holy Spirit* by Billy Graham, and *By the Power of the Holy Spirit* by David Howard.

# EIGHT

# Jesus: The Spirit of Truth

*John 15:18—16:33; 1 John 4:1-6*

## Objectives

1. To recognize the choice which must be made between following Jesus Christ or following the world, between listening to the Spirit of Truth or listening to the spirit of falsehood.

2. To understand how we can test the spirits as we are told to do in 1 John 4:1.

3. To perceive the work of the Holy Spirit within us and know that he is "greater than the one who is in the world."

## Background Information

*The meaning of truth:* Carved in stone above the entrance to the administration building of the University of Texas are the words of Jesus: "You will know the truth, and the truth will set you free." It is doubtful if many who pass through those doors realize that Jesus put a qualification before that statement. John records both in his Gospel, 8:31, 32. "*If* you hold to my teaching, you are really my disciples. *Then* you will know the truth, and the truth will set you free." Jesus promised knowledge of truth only to those who hold to his teaching.

This is easy to understand when we remember what we've already learned about truth in John's works:

Truth is found in Jesus Christ. *John 1:14*
Truth comes to us through Jesus. *John 1:17*
Truth is taught by Jesus. *John 5:24, 25*
Truth is Jesus Christ. *John 14:6*
Truth now comes to us through the guidance and help of the Spirit of truth, sent by Jesus Christ. *John 14:16, 17; 16:13*
Truth is essential to our worship of God. *John 4:24*
Truth can be known and will set us free. *John 8:31, 32*
Truth must be our guide for living. *John 3:21*
Truth is not our guide and is not in us
if we walk in darkness, *1 John 1:6*
if we don't acknowledge our sin, *1 John 1:8*
if we don't obey God. *1 John 2:4*
Truth is in us and has hold of our lives
if our hearts don't condemn us. *1 John 3:19-22*

John makes a clear division between those who belong to the world and those who belong to Christ. Those who are against Christ (antichrists) speak from the viewpoint of the world (1 John 4:5) and are guided by the spirit of falsehood (1 John 4:6). Those who belong to Christ know God, and are guided by the Spirit of truth (John 8:31, 32; 16:13).

*The firm foundation in the God of truth:* How can we abide in the truth and not be misled by the spirit of falsehood?

1. We can build our lives on a solid foundation. In 1 Samuel 2:2 Hannah says in her prayer, "There is no Rock like our God." Later King David sang, "The Lord is my rock, my fortress and my deliverer; my God is my rock, in whom I take refuge" (Psalm 18:2). In 1 Corinthians 10:1-13 Paul identifies Jesus Christ as the spiritual rock upon whom the forefathers of the Christian faith depended. In these verses Paul points out the failures of the Israelites because they did not cling to the Rock, but rather chose to go the ways of the world. He encourages believers to stand firm in Christ Jesus and trust a faithful God who will provide the help we need.

2. We can study God's Word knowing that it contains truth

(2 Timothy 3:14-17). The answers to all our questions and all our problems are in Scripture.

3. We can listen to the Holy Spirit within us. Jesus sent the Holy Spirit to keep us from error and to guide us into all truth (John 16:13, 14).

## Visual Aids

1. To begin the lesson, you may wish to have the Scripture passages pertaining to "truth" (background information: The meaning of truth) printed on poster paper, written on a chalkboard, or mimeographed.

2. Print the following verse on poster paper and place it in a prominent place in the room:

*You belong to God and have already won your fight with those who are against Christ, because there is someone in your hearts who is stronger than any evil teacher in this wicked world.*

1 John 4:4 (TLB)

# NINE

# Jesus: Perfect Love

*John 17:1—18:27; 1 John 4:7-21*

## Objectives

1. To see the love of Jesus as he prays for himself, for the disciples, and for all future believers.

2. To explore the meaning of "glory" as it relates to Jesus and to us.

3. To sense, as Peter did, what it means to deny Jesus, who loves us perfectly.

4. To see more clearly what it means to be loved of God and what it means to love one another.

## Background Information

*The Lord's Prayer:* On Thursday evening following the celebration of the Passover Feast with his disciples, the washing of their feet, and the promise of the Holy Spirit, Jesus lifted his eyes toward heaven and prayed. John does not tell us where Jesus was when he prayed, apparently not considering the place to be important.

Today we call John 17 the Lord's Prayer. It is in three parts: (1) In verses 1-5, Jesus prays for himself; (2) in verses 6-19, Jesus prays for the disciples; and (3) in verses 20-26, Jesus prays for all future believers.

*Glory:* The theme of the first part of the Lord's Prayer is "glory," and the word appears again in parts 2 and 3. John speaks of two kinds of glory: that which Jesus received while on earth and is to be shared with men (verses 1, 4, 22), and that which is reserved for the Father, Son, and Holy Spirit and is visible only in heaven (verses 5, 24). We can share in the first kind of glory because our works glorify Christ (15:8). But the second kind of glory we will only behold when we get to heaven (17:24).

If you wish to do a study of "glory" or "glorify" as it is used in John's Gospel (NIV), the following references will help: 1:14; 2:11; 7:39; 8:50, 54; 11:4, 40; 12:16, 23, 28, 41; 13:31, 32; 14:13; 15:8; 16:14; 17:1, 4, 5, 10, 22, 24; 21:19.

*Denying Jesus:* The seriousness of Peter's denial of Jesus (18:15-27) can be seen more clearly if it is viewed in light of Jesus' teaching in Mark 8:27-38. While his denial is a human failing, Peter is none the less held accountable. His denial demands repentance and forgiveness. Later, in John 21:15-19, we will see Jesus lovingly bring Peter to this understanding.

## Visual Aids

Type out 1 John 4:7-21, double-spaced, with wide margins on top, bottom, and sides. It isn't necessary to indent for paragraphs or to number verses, but numbering every fifth line in the left margin will be helpful. Mimeograph enough copies of this manuscript so that each member of the group can have one. Have pencils or pens on hand.

To begin your lesson in 1 John, ask members of the group to read through their manuscripts and circle the word "love" each time it appears (twenty-five times). This will move you into a discussion of love: definition, giver, receiver.

Next, ask members to underline all phrases which begin with the preposition "in" ("in him," "in us," "in God," "in love"). This will lead to a discussion of what each of these phrases means.

# TEN

# The New Birth: Victory in Christ

*John 18:28—20:10; 1 John 5:1-12*

## Objectives

1. To understand the guilt of mankind as revealed in Pilate and the soldiers (gentiles) and the Jews who rejected Jesus.

2. To see Jesus' death as the fulfilling of God's plan to save mankind.

3. To see our new birth in Christ as a victory over death won for us by Jesus Christ.

## Background Information

*Cross:* Execution in the Old Testament was by stoning, not crucifixion; however, dead bodies of Jews guilty of idolatry and blasphemy were sometimes hung on trees as a warning to others. Always these bodies were considered cursed and had to be taken down and buried before sundown. The Romans adopted the practice of crucifixion from the Phoenicians but reserved this punishment for slaves, provincials, and the worst criminals—rarely for their citizens. These known practices must have added to Christ's deep humiliation and shame.

But the cross in the New Testament is more than a symbol of

shame imposed by man on our Lord. Christ "humbled himself and became obedient to death—even death on a cross" (Phil. 2:8). He bore the sin and punishment of all mankind and gave his "life as a ransom for many" (Matthew 20:28). Hebrews 9:22 tells us that "without the shedding of blood, there is no forgiveness." Christ died on the cross, but he was victorious over death—physical and spiritual death. He arose a conqueror. It is in this fact that the total sufficiency of Christ to save us and give us eternal life rests.

### Visual Aids

1. Have two crosses sitting on a table—one a cross with Jesus hanging there, the other one empty. The first cross will remind the group of Jesus' suffering and death for our sins. The second will remind the group of Jesus' victory over sin and death. Discuss the importance of understanding the truths behind the symbols of both crosses.
2. The following poems can be found in almost any good collection of English literature. You may wish to use one or more of them at an appropriate place in the lesson. "The Lord Turned, and Looked upon Peter," by Elizabeth Barrett Browning; "Pilate Remembers," "Herod Plans," and "Barabbas," by William E. Brooks; "A Guard of the Sepulcher," by Edwin Markham.

# ELEVEN

# Jesus: Our Way, Our Truth, Our Life

*John 20:11—21:25; 1 John 5:13-21*

## Objectives

1. To know that Jesus is the Christ, the Son of God, and our way to the Father.
2. To know that we are in him who is truth.
3. To know that in him we have eternal life.

## Background Information

*Resurrection:* The Old Testament does not give much attention to resurrection of individuals. However, such Scripture verses as Job 19:25-27, Ecclesiastes 3:21 and 12:7, Isaiah 25:8 and Daniel 12:13, clearly testify to a belief in resurrection. The New Testament is filled with teaching about our resurrection, and the book of Revelation details the last days. Jesus assured us in John 5:24-29 and 11:25 of the resurrection of all mankind—some to eternal life and others to condemnation.

At the time of Christ, most Jews, with the exception of the Sadducees who denied all teachings of life after death, believed that their same bodies without change would be brought back to life. Greeks believed that the soul was immortal but the body would perish.

The early Christian view of the resurrection differed from both Jewish and Greek beliefs. Because Christ's body was resurrected from the dead, Christians understood that their bodies, too, would be raised. But because Christ's body was transformed to be more useful in a life to come, they also believed their bodies would be transformed. This view is accepted by most Christians today.

In 1 Corinthians 15, Paul talks about the importance of the resurrection to the Christian faith and gives us additional understanding of what our resurrection bodies will be like.

### Visual Aids

1. Read the following poem, "St. John, The Aged," and discuss the reactions of the group to the poet's perception of John's death. This may lead to a discussion of how they feel about death.

2. Part III of Handel's *Messiah* begins with, "I know that my Redeemer liveth." Locate a good recording and play this at the end of your lesson.

## ST. JOHN, THE AGED
Author Unknown

*I'm growing very old. This weary head*
*That hath so often leaned on Jesus' breast,*
*In days long past that seem almost a dream,*
*Is bent and hoary with its weight of years.*
*These limbs that followed Him—my Master—oft*
*From Galilee to Judah; yea, that stood*
*Beneath the cross, and trembled with His groans,*
*Refuse to bear me even through the streets*
*To preach unto my children. E'en my lips*
*Refuse to form the words my heart sends forth.*
*My ears are dull, they scarcely hear the sobs*
*Of my dear children gathered round my couch;*
*God lays His hand upon me—yea, His hand!*
*And not His rod—the gentle hand that I*
*Felt, those three years, so often pressed in mine,*
*In friendship such as passeth woman's love.*
*I'm old, so old I cannot recollect*
*The faces of my friends; and I forget*
*The words and deeds that make up daily life;*
*But that dear face, and every word He spoke,*
*Grow more distinct as others fade away,*
*So that I live with Him and holy dead*
*More than with living.*

*Some seventy years ago*
*I was a fisher by the sacred sea.*
*It was at sunset. How the tranquil tide*
*Bathed dreamily the pebbles. How the light*
*Crept up the distant hills and in its wake*
*Soft purple shadows wrapped the dewy fields.*
*And then He came and called me. Then I gazed,*
*For the first time, as from a window, shone*
*Divinity, looked on the inmost soul,*
*Broke on the silence of my heart and made*
*The whole world musical. Incarnate Love*
*Took hold of me and claimed me for its own.*

*I followed in the twilight, holding fast*
*His mantle.*

*O what holy walks we had,*
*Through harvest fields, and desolate dreary wastes,*
*And oftentimes He leaned upon my arm,*
*Wearied and wayworn; I was young and strong*
*And so upbore Him. Lord, now I am weak,*
*And old, and feeble. Let me rest on Thee.*
*How strong Thou art. The twilight draws apace.*
*Come, let us leave these noisy streets and take*
*The path to Bethany; for Mary's smile*
*Awaits us at the gate, and Martha's hands*
*Have long prepared the cheerful evening meal.*
*Come, James, the Master waits; and, Peter, see,*
*Has gone some steps before.*

*What say you, Friends?*
*That this is Ephesus? Aye, 'tis so, 'tis so,*
*I know it all; and yet, just now, I seemed*
*To stand once more upon my native hills,*
*The touch of His garments brings back strength*
*To palsied limbs. I feel it has to mine.*
*Up! bear me once more to my church. Once more*
*There let me tell you of a Saviour's love:*
*For, by the sweetness of my Master's voice*
*Just now, I think He must be very near—*
*Coming, I trust, to break the veil, which time*
*Has worn so thin that I can see beyond*
*And watch His footsteps.*

*So raise up my head.*
*How dark it is! I cannot seem to see*
*The face of my flock. Is that the sea*
*That murmurs so, or is it weeping? Hush,*
*My little children. God so loved the world,*
*He gave His Son. So love ye one another:*
*Love God and man. Amen. Now bear me back.*
*My legacy unto an angry world is that.*

*I feel my work is finished. Are the streets so full?*
*What, call the folk my name? The Holy John?*
*Nay, write me rather Jesus Christ's beloved,*
*And lover of my children.*

*Lay me down*
*Once more upon my couch, and open wide*
*The eastern window. See, there comes a light*
*Like that which broke upon my soul at eve,*
*When, in the dreary isle of Patmos, Gabriel came,*
*And touched me upon the shoulder. See, it grows,*
*As when He mounted toward the pearly gates.*
*I know the way. I trod it once before.*
*And hark! It is the song the ransomed sang*
*Of glory to the Lamb. How loud it sounds.*
*And that unwritten one. Me thinks my soul*
*Can join it now. But who are these who crowd*
*The shining way? Say—joy! 'Tis the eleven,*
*With Peter first. How eagerly he looks.*
*How bright the smiles are beaming on James' face.*
*I am the last. Once more we are complete,*
*To gather round the Paschal feast. My place*
*Is next my Master. O my Lord, my Lord,*
*How bright Thou art, and yet the very same*
*I loved in Galilee. 'Tis worth the hundred years*
*To feel this bliss. So, lift me up, dear Lord,*
*Unto Thy bosom. There shall I abide.*

## Suggested References

Bruce, F. F. *New Testament History*. Garden City, N. Y.: Oliphants and Doubleday, 1971.

*Everyday Life in Bible Times*. New York: National Geographic Society, 1976.

*Great People of the Bible and How They Lived*. Pleasantville, N. Y.: Reader's Digest Association, Inc., 1979.

Guthrie, Donald. *New Testament Introduction*. Downers Grove, Ill.: InterVarsity Press, 1973.

Guthrie, Donald, and J. A. Motyer, eds. *The New Bible Commentary*, rev. ed. Grand Rapids, Mich.: Eerdmans Pub., 1970.

Harrison, Everett F. *Introduction to the New Testament*, rev. ed. Grand Rapids, Mich.: Eerdmans, 1964.

Henry, Matthew. *Understanding the Gospel of John*. Old Tappan, N. J.: Fleming H. Revell Co., n.d.

*The Illustrated Bible Dictionary*. 3 vols. Wheaton, Ill.: Tyndale House, 1981.

Keller, Werner. *The Bible as History*. New York: Wm. Morrow and Co., 1964.

Mould, Elmer W. K. *Essentials of Bible History*. New York: Ronald Press, 1951.

*Oxford Bible Atlas*. Oxford, England: Oxford Univ. Press, 1974.

Packer, James I., Merrill C. Tenney and William White, Jr. *The Bible Almanac*. Nashville, Tenn.: Thomas Nelson Pub., 1980.

Tenney, Merrill C. *New Testament Survey*. Grand Rapids, Mich.: Eerdmans, 1961.

Young, Robert. *Analytical Concordance to the Bible*. New York: Funk and Wagnalls, n.d.